Be BAD!

Blessed, Anointed, and Delivered Through Prayer

Phyllis Thomas

Second Edition

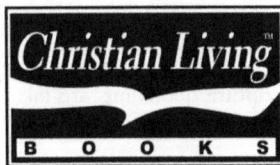

Christian Living™

B O O K S

Christian Living Books, Inc.
Largo, MD

ISBN 9781562293789

Christian Living Books, Inc.
P. O. Box 7584
Largo, MD 20792
christianlivingbooks.com
We bring your dreams to fruition.

Unless otherwise noted, Scripture quotations are taken from the King James Version of the Bible.

Printed in the United States of America.

ENDORSEMENTS

*T*his book is a practical masterpiece that will provoke a desire within you to develop a more intimate relationship with God through prayer. Lady Thomas, whose brilliance is upstaged by her integrity and graciousness, has written this very simple book. It will teach, encourage, and inspire you to communicate with God on a more personal and divine level. Each chapter provides you with thought-provoking, biblical insight, personal experience, and spiritual elements to access God through prayer. Whether you are new to the faith or have been serving in God's Kingdom for years, your prayer life will never be the same after reading this book.

Phonechia Thomas-Harrison
Clinical Specialist
Mercy Hospital

Be BAD! is a power-packed, strategic manual for prayer! Lady Thomas teaches the essential components for Christian living. Hers is a personal, yet sundry approach that anyone, at any level in their walk, can relate to. Introspective and insightful, Lady Thomas narrates a stirring, yet moving journey filled with both laughter and tears. This book will change you!

Cynthia Alexander
Youth Ministry and Marketing Consultant
Liberty Church

Anyone who underestimates who they are in Christ or how important having a prayer life is should read this book. Lady Thomas strategically unveils how to develop a strong prayer life that will equip you to overcome the fiery darts of the enemy and draw closer to God. Utilizing the spiritual insight in this book will help you to realize what it means to be Blessed, Anointed, and Delivered.

Dr. Symone Starr Parker
Business Professor
University of Phoenix

At the ripe age of thirty, I was 430 pounds, battling internal demons, suffering from insecurities, and seeking validation in all the wrong places! Author, Motivator, Pastor's Wife, Mother, but most of all, Woman of God, Lady Thomas is a walking example of the healing agent I desperately needed. That is clearly demonstrated in this book! Why? The answer is very simple; she is "BAD."

If you are looking for a life-changing and personal transformation, built on a foundation that can't fail, this is the book! If you are ready to deal with and remove the layers and years of hidden pain, YOU MUST read this book! If you are ready to invest in your worth and seek validation from GOD, then this is your book!

The golden jewels tied to each short story reflecting the personal turning points Lady Thomas captured are handcrafted and tailor-made for this generation. Most importantly, the Word of God, the healing agent prescribed in this book, is captured with great wisdom. You will read and experience the strategic application of the Word at work, which will only set you up to WIN and of course, "Be BAD"!

J. D. Gunn
Senior Manager of Performance Intelligence
Centene Corporation

This is a great read! I could not put it down! *Be BAD* offers a profound yet practical approach to reaching the throne of God through prayer. Chapter two reveals, 'When you pray, no fancy or formalized words are required.' How wonderful it is to know that eloquence in speech is not a prerequisite to God hearing and answering prayer. The only necessity is to just pray and be BAD.

Evangelist Michelle Perkins

Lady Thomas is truly BAD (Blessed. Anointed. Delivered). I would dare say that she is REAL BAD, not only in terms of being a sincere individual but REAL as in a Respectful. Extraordinary. Authentic. Laborer (for God). Her words written, match her words spoken, and are evident in her life. I have had the privilege of having her as my First Lady and have worked with her in the business arena as well. She is the same in the pulpit as she is on the pavement, truly driven by prayer and led by God. She tarries in deep communion with Him and often feasts on His Word as she waits to hear His voice. She's not only built a close relationship with Him, but she has helped others experience Him on a deeper level. She is not selfish in her anointing. She pours out fervent prayers for others as God has poured into her. This book will make

the word "BAD" good while making you great. So, get ready
to strut in the promise and bring others with you.

Samantha Moorer

Vice Principal

Be BAD! is a must read! This book will challenge those seeking a transformational experience in their spiritual life of
disciplines.

Dr. Beverly Willis

ACKNOWLEDGMENTS

I thank God, the Author and Finisher of my faith, for giving me this opportunity to share my spiritual experiences with the body of Christ.

To my wonderful husband, Pastor Darnell Thomas, thank you for your unfailing love, your words of encouragement and your continuous support. Thank you for being my #1 fan. I love you, Sunshine, forever and a day!

To my mother, Esther Thompson, thank you for teaching me the importance of putting God first and for instilling the value of prayer in me at a very young age. I love you, Mom!

To my Showers of Blessings spiritual family, thank you for all your prayers, love, support, and inspiration.

CONTENTS

BE BAD!
PRAYER JOURNAL

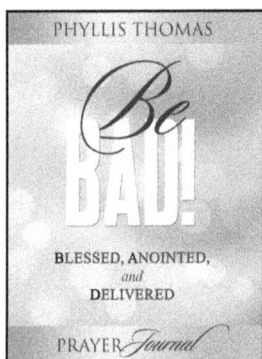

*D*evelop the tools that empower you to be BAD! With this journal praying, reading the Bible, and hearing from God will become your lifestyle, not rituals. It is designed to stimulate your thoughts, cause you to reflect, and motivate you to action. Each day you use this resource you build your spiritual muscles. Before you know it, with the daily Bible reading chart, you will have covered the entire Bible. The Prayer Journal includes...

- A monthly topic, scripture, prayer, and challenge
- Thoughtful questions to help you process and keep you engaged
- A daily checklist to keep you on track
- A read the Bible in a year chart
- A-Z affirmations and prayers
- Answered prayer chart

Let the power of Spirit-led prayer, journaling, and affirmations create your new reality. Do the work to develop great habits and a healthy spiritual life. Whether it's for personal worship, or group study, this is the perfect resource to build a stronger relationship with Christ!

ISBN 9781562293772 | 8.5"x11" | Paperback | 96 pages
Available wherever books are sold or from ChristianLivingBooks.com

FOREWORD

*H*ow many of you have said to yourself, "Lord, if I could just move forward from being stuck in this mentality of defeat, negativity, depression, and self-pity"? Many are hostages to their own reality, without the resources nor spiritual guidance to help them on their journey to freedom and wholeness.

The enemy is devising plans to literally destroy the minds of people. Why? The enemy is aware that his days are short on the earth; therefore, he works relentlessly to stop believers in Jesus Christ. He realizes that the believer is a threat to his kingdom. He desires to stop the believer by any means necessary. The Word of God declares that *The thief cometh not, but for to steal, and to kill, and to destroy: I am come that they might have life, and that they might have it more abundantly.* (John 10:10). You see, we can choose to live in abundance – which is a promise by God – or to allow the enemy to continue to steal, kill, and destroy us. I encourage you to choose wisely.

While reading this explosive book, I was really thinking. My initial thoughts were of gratitude. I started praising God by faith that souls will be transformed while reading this practical book. It is packed with self-defeating paradigms and examples to compare your own life situations to. I admire Lady Thomas for so transparently expressing examples from her own life such as challenges, stressors, delusions and snares of the enemy – one being depression. Thank you, Jesus, for breakthrough prayer.

The keys, building blocks, and action plan Lady Thomas uses so intelligently serve as models for us to grow from. She testifies and honors God for being her source of strength and deliverance while recognizing that prayer equipped her to do what honors the Lord the most. She is indeed a woman of grace. Her walk demonstrates to all that know her the benefits of having a constant prayer life. Her life is a reflection of prayer and fasting which enable her to walk in authority with a determination to equip those that struggle in different areas. Lady Thomas carefully and purposefully reminds the reader that prayer is the source of having a victorious life. Ask yourself, "Are you ready to live?" If so, move forward and be BAD.

To be BAD, you must do the work. Through prayer, you will learn how to respond without negative reactions to the designs, plots, tricks, and plans of the enemy. You must be in a position to fight. How do you fight? You use the Word of God, for the Word works. Lady Thomas strategically gives the reader the tools to fight. She equips with information and wisdom on how to go in prayer and come out as a BAD soldier of Jesus Christ.

Use this book as a means of empowering yourself to be transformed through the Word of God. Take the golden nuggets from this book and challenge yourself to ascend in your prayer life. Welcome each word you read and meditate on the insights as it ministers to your soul, and strengthens you to stand in times of adversity and pain. I declare that you are BAD in God. Do the work to be a better you. Read intently and know that there is spiritual wealth in the secret place.

Lady Vicki L. Kemp
Author of the bestselling book, *Better than Yesterday*

CHAPTER 1

WHAT IS BEING BAD?

And he spake a parable unto to them to this end, that men ought always to pray and not to faint. (Luke 18:1)

*A*re you wondering what it means to be BAD? Do you want to know why I want you to be BAD when you were taught all your life to be good? The answer is simple. God wants you to be BAD too. It is His plan, purpose, and will for you. In fact, being BAD is great! It is a way of living that will change you forever. So be BAD – Blessed, Anointed, and Delivered through the power of prayer.

I know there are lots of prayer books and many prayer journals on the market, but this book will encourage, inspire, and challenge you to action. You will plant a seed that will grow and make you BAD through prayer. Consequently, the power of prayer will move God into action on your behalf.

The Spirit of God inspired me to write this book as I was praying one morning around 6:00 A.M. God does not always speak audibly; sometimes He brings clear, pure thoughts to your mind as a form of speaking. That's what He did with me.

The Spirit of the Lord said to me, "You are bad."

Well, needless to say, my response was, "Lord, I know I'm not the best person in the world but *bad*? Wow! That hits pretty deep."

Then the Lord said to me, "Why not ask Me what I mean?"

Of course, I was curious. What did God mean when He said I was bad? I mustered enough courage to ask Him, but He repeated the same three words to me, "You are bad."

I said, "Alright Lord, what do You mean I'm bad?"

He responded, "You are My *blessed, anointed,* and *delivered* child."

Of course, I praised God as if I had just been handed a million dollars. I walked around saying to myself, "I'm BAD. I'm BAD. I'm BAD." You see, what I realized at that point was that it was the Spirit and power of God behind those letters – BAD (blessed, anointed, delivered).

CALLED TO PRAYER

I'm BAD, and I know I'm BAD because I am a prayer warrior for Jesus. I was called to the ministry of prayer according to my Savior before my mother conceived me. God knew who He called me to be, what He called me to do, and where He would take me to do battle for Him in prayer. He also knew exactly how I would get there. The power of prayer keeps me BAD. Prayer helped me realize who I am and whose I am.

How about you? Do you know who you are and whose you are? You can be successful on this journey, but you must be BAD through the power of prayer.

You picked up this book actually looking for an answer to some of life's difficulties. I assure you, you will find it through the awesome power of prayer. In this book, I will share some of my experiences with you. I hope to convince you of the benefits and power found in communicating with God continually.

> *May you commit to a life of power and prayer.*

MY PRAYER FOR YOU

Heavenly Father, I come boldly before the throne of Your grace in humility. As Your BAD child, I beseech You to look upon the readers of this book with Your divine favor. Let Your Holy Spirit rest upon them now, and allow them to experience the sweet aroma of Your presence overshadowing them. Give them peace that surpasses all understanding along with joy unspeakable. Replace their wisdom with Your wisdom and their understanding with Your understanding. Manifest Yourself to them in a miraculous way as they commit themselves to You in prayer. Let Your blessings shower down on them and overflow every part of their being. Meet their needs spiritually, physically, mentally, and financially. Give them mindsets to be BAD through communicating with You. Open their spiritual eyes that they may see and their spiritual ears that they may hear. Give them the wisdom and knowledge to understand Your written Word, rightly divide Your truth and apply Your Word to their lives daily. Help them to know the authority they have over Satan and teach them how to combat every demonic force that comes against them. Help them to realize that greater is He (God) who is in them than he (devil) that is in the world. Help them to know that no matter what comes or goes, no weapon formed against them will prosper. Lord, keep Your praises carved on their lips and songs of praise ringing in their hearts as they exalt, magnify, and glorify You. All of these things I ask in the name of Your Son, Jesus. It shall be done. Amen!

Wow! I believe you are ready to become that BAD servant through the power of prayer.

REMEMBER – YOU ARE BAD! SO STAY BAD!

CHAPTER 2

THE VALUE OF PRAYER

Pray without ceasing. (1 Thessalonians 5:17)

*P*rayer is an earnest request made to God. It is a channel by which communication occurs between God and mankind. Prayer is an essential tool to receive direction and to keep a connection with God. Daily communication with God has such immense value you must take hold of every opportunity to pray and let Him download His desires into your spirit.

Prayer is also a ministry that should be desired and developed. It is a prescription for any hurt, pain or problem. Moreover, it is one of the best weapons against the satanic attacks, traps, and adversities sent by the devil.

Value is the worth or importance of something to its possessor. Our prayers are so valuable that Revelations 5:8 says the prayers of the saints are kept in golden vials. If you value prayer, doing it should be a daily routine just like putting on clothes.

The value of prayer reveals that there is enough power to heal, give peace, deliver, comfort, and set a person free. You don't need fancy or formalized words to pray. Rather, a pure heart, a reverential approach, and a positive attitude are the keys to unlocking the door of God's heart. God enjoys communicating with His children.

> The sacrifice of the wicked is an abomination to the Lord; but the prayer of the upright is His delight. (Proverbs 15:8)

Throughout the Bible, there are various scriptures, which point to the fact that God wants us to pray. In Luke 18:1, Jesus says, "Men (mankind) ought always to pray, and not to faint." When life is all out of whack, prayer is always in order, and it will help put things back on track.

HOW DO I BEGIN TO PRAY?

Start right now – at this very moment. Make a commitment to talk to God daily. When I teach on prayer, I always challenge people to take 15 minutes of quality time a day for 21 days to pray (don't miss a day). Then I encourage them to watch the change that will take place in their lives. Those 15 minutes will turn into 30 minutes and eventually, it becomes an hour. That quality time will continue to increase to the point that prayer becomes a habit. It becomes addictive. Actually, praying is the best form of addiction to have in this world today.

You begin praying by first realizing how essential prayer is in your walk with God. With that in mind, acknowledge the majesty, deity, magnificence, character, and glory of the almighty God. God's very nature and attributes exceed those of the most prominent or renowned human beings. Therefore, giving God recognition and His props is really how you begin to pray. In a relationship, you express your love to the person you are with. You tell that person how much you love him or her and what you love about him or her. In the same manner, you are to communicate your love to God. You must adore and appreciate Him more than the person you are in love with. As you acknowledge God's sovereignty, you exalt Him as having supreme power, rank, and authority above anything or anyone else in this world.

How do you begin? You pray with sincerity and humility in faith and in the name of Jesus.

Make a commitment to talk to God daily.

> And whatsoever ye shall ask in my name, that will I do that the Father may be glorified in the Son. If ye shall ask anything in my name, I will do it. (John 14:13-14)

When you pray by faith in the name of Jesus according to His divine will, expect to receive what you have asked for. Then with patience, wait on the positive results.

THE BUILDING BLOCKS

Developing your prayer life entails seeking greater intimacy with God. Your prayers should incorporate the following:

19

- ***Adoration*** – This is the act of worship. It is profound love or regard. Praise God for His greatness and goodness (Psalm 150)
- ***Thanksgiving*** – The outpouring of gratitude to God because of His grace, mercy, lovingkindness, and favor toward you (Psalm 103:1-5)
- ***Confession*** – The acknowledgment of any sin committed (1 John 1:9)
- ***Petition*** – A plea for personal help, care, love, strength, and power (Philippians 4:6)
- ***Intercession*** – The earnest request or petition in favor of another (1 Timothy 2:1)
- ***Submission*** – The abandonment of your own desires. The surrender of your will to God's will (James 4:7). When you submit yourself in prayer, you enter the presence of God surrendering your entire being to His will and workings in your life

As you begin to flow through each of those categories, your awareness of who God really is heightens. Furthermore, you will see yourself and your shortcomings. Such consciousness will push you to be a better individual who perseveres to become all God has designed you to be.

I've learned that you can pray the scriptures. For instance, you can say to God:

> Lord, let the words of my mouth and the meditation of my heart be acceptable in your sight today because you are my strength and my redeemer. (Psalm 19:14)

A TO Z

You can also pray to God using the alphabet from A to Z. All you need to do is get a dictionary and look up words that you want to use to adore God. I enjoy praying to God using the alphabet. My prayer goes a little like this:

A – God You are an awesome God. You are the all-knowing God.

B – God You are the best thing that has ever happened to me. You are so beautiful to me.

C – Thank You, Lord, for being such a caring God. You are always concerned about me.

D – Thank You for being my divine Savior and for showing me such grace and mercy.

E – Thank You for being effective in my life. You are excellent, extra-special, and extraordinary in all that You do for me.

F – You are a faithful God, a fantastic God.

G – You are a gracious and good God.

H – Thank You, Lord, for being so helpful and giving me hope. You are a holy God, a heavenly God. Most of all, You are a habit-forming God.

I – You are the inspiration for my soul. You illuminate me with Your spiritual power, blocking out the shadow of darkness generated by the devil.

J – You are my joy in sorrow. You are a just God.

K – Thank You for Your kindness; it is more than anyone could ever give.

L – You are loving, loyal, and the reason I am living.

M – You are magnificent, marvelous, and the mover of obstacles on my behalf.

N – You are a nice God. You are a numinous (supernatural) God, a right-now God. You are number one to me.

O – You are an omnipotent, omniscient, and omnipresent God. There is none like You.

P – You are a powerful and patient God. You are my peace and my problem-solver.

Q – Your attributes radiate the character of quintessence (pureness). You quench my spiritual thirst like no one else can.

R – You are a righteous God, a God I respect and reverence. You are my source of direction when I need it.

S – You are my Savior, sanctifier, and satisfier. You are so sweet to me.

T – You are a trustworthy God. You are always true to Your Word. You are absolutely terrific.

U – When I think of You, Lord, I thank You for Your understanding, for being unique and unchangeable.

V – Thank You for being my very present help in times of trouble. You are so versatile.

W – Wonderful You are and a watchman over my soul. I desire with my whole heart to gain wisdom from You.

X – You are the X-rayer of my soul.

Y – You are my yesterday, today, and forever. You are just yummy to me.

Z – Thank You for being my zest for life. I appreciate You always zooming in on my needs.

Praying using the alphabet will render about 15 to 20 minutes or more of adoration and thanksgiving to the Master. Take a moment to experience the excitement as you seek the most valuable words to express your love for God.

THE BENEFITS

In my quest to encourage you to become BAD in prayer, I want you to know there are many benefits prayer provides. Prayer is a guiding source of vision, power, strength, direction, creativity, and blessings for your life. Ultimate relief is received through sincere prayer. The benefit of prayer that I enjoy is the fact that it brings me into the presence of God. That keeps me focused on His plan, purpose, and will for my life. Those benefits are also available to you. You can find encouragement and comfort in prayer – what a benefit! Prayer will influence you to do the will of God and direct you to always give glory to Him for all He does.

If you ever need an answer to any of life's situations, I guarantee you will receive a response when you pray.

Do you want to be blessed, anointed, and delivered (BAD)? Value the art of prayer and watch a spiritual explosion take place. It happened to me, and I love it!

MY PRAYER FOR YOU

Lord, teach all those who read this book to value their relationship with You. Give them insight into who You are and how wonderful You are as they become consistent in communicating with You. Show them Your ways and teach them Your paths that they may experience the manifestation of Your matchless power. Give them a hunger and thirst to adore and praise You as King of kings and Lord of lords. Bless them in all their efforts as they endeavor to enrich their spiritual man through prayer. In Jesus' name, I pray. Amen!

CHAPTER 3

BLESSED FOR SERVICE

Blessed are they which do hunger and thirst after righteousness: for they shall be filled. (Matthew 5:6)

*W*hat comes to your mind when you think of the word
"blessed"? Do you think about your status in life? Do you
measure how many material, earthly treasures you've gained?

Your position (status) in life, your material possessions – big or
small – are blessings. However, they do not necessarily reflect
that you are blessed. The scriptural meaning of "blessed" is to
be happy. You may have all the fame and fortune yet not be
blessed (happy). Being blessed is a characteristic that is displayed in your relationship with God. You may not have earthly
fame and wealth but having a personal one-on-one relationship
with the Creator produces the type of happiness to be valued.

In the sense of performing duties for God, service is an act of
devotion to Him. We are to be happy (blessed) in our service

(devotion) to God as we demonstrate our love for Him. "How do we do this?" you may ask. We do this by obeying His instructions.

EARLY MORNING PRAYER

Allow me to tell you how I became blessed for service. In 1983, the Spirit of the Lord spoke to me and said that He wanted me to attend 6:00 A.M. prayer at my local church. Well, my first reaction was, "Lord, that's awfully early." The Holy Spirit went on to tell me how I would be blessed and how prayer would be beneficial to me and others. The Spirit of the Lord also said that I had a "call" to prayer; in fact, It was my ministry. Of course, I tried to find a later time in the day that I could pray. Plus, I made excuses like these:

1. It's too early, and I'm going to be extremely tired.

2. I may fall asleep during prayer.

3. I have to be at work by 7:30 A.M.

4. That area by the railroad tracks can be dangerous.

5. I don't think I can pray for a full hour.

What's so interesting about God is that He will let you say all that you're going to say. Then He addresses each of your concerns (excuses). These are the Lord's comments to each one of my excuses:

1. Your night schedule will have to change. Instead of watching television until 11:00 P.M. or midnight, you'll have to

retire no later than 9:30 P.M. Prepare yourself for the following day, and it won't take you as long to get dressed.

2. Even if you fall asleep, at least, you're in My presence, and you won't be asleep for long. I will see to that.

3. It will only take you 15 minutes to drive from the church to your job, park your car, and walk into the building. You will still have 15 minutes to spare.

4. My Word states that My angels encamp around about you (Psalm 34:7). Don't worry; don't be afraid. I will protect you from danger – seen and unseen.

5. Trust Me! I will teach you how to pray.

After those responses, I still wanted God to confirm to me that it was Him speaking and directing me to attend the 6:00 A.M. prayer service (like the devil was going to tell me to pray – I don't think so!).

> *The scriptural meaning of "blessed" is to be happy.*

My pastor at the time was an older gentleman. We affectionately called him Dad. Dad was a man of wisdom, charm, and understanding; he always displayed his love for young people. The following Sunday (after I asked the Lord for confirmation) directly after Sunday school, Dad motioned for me to come to the podium area where he was sitting. He told me to have a seat. He looked at me and explained that the prayer leader for the 6:00 A.M. prayer time would be leaving the ministry to go and assist her brother who was just beginning his duties as a pastor. After providing me this information, he proceeded to tell me that the Lord told him to have me take over the prayer leader role for the 6:00 A.M. prayer. He then paused, looked at me and said, "Will you do it?" My response was, "Sure, Pastor, I will do it." Of course, when I went back to my seat, I was blown away by God's quick confirmation of my prayer. Additionally, what magnified God's confirmation was Pastor's announcement to the congregation that I was now in charge of the 6:00 A.M. prayer service.

My first time leading the early morning prayer session was quite easy because I was the only one there. I entered the sanctuary, knelt down and said, "Lord, it's me and You. Please, teach me how to pray." From that moment, I began to develop my relationship with God in prayer; it has changed my life completely. My life of prayer has been so beneficial to me that when problems arise, I don't seek the advice of others. I immediately go to God in prayer.

For many weeks and months, I met God at 6:00 A.M... alone. For a total of nine years, I was the 6:00 A.M. prayer leader. The hunger and thirst for more of God were embedded in me during my nine-year journey. Even today, God and I still have our special, quality time together. It continues to be an awesome experience with Him. All of the answers to any questions I have are provided during my daily meditation and devotions with God. Even at my lowest of lows, I receive enlightenment during prayer.

Prayer ministry is my life. I get such relief, refreshment, joy, and peace when I pray. Praying makes me happy (blessed). I get excited just talking about it because I know the power of prayer, and I want you to experience it too. If you want to be blessed, dedicate yourself to prayer.

BLESSED TO SERVE

The other fantastic benefit of prayer is serving others by interceding on their behalf. I am elated to see God manifest Himself in other people's lives and change their circumstances. You will be overjoyed because you touched and agreed with that person for God to move. What an awesome experience to watch God unfold His handiwork of resolution in other's lives when we obey the Holy One and pray.

You are blessed to serve. Whether you serve others through prayer or a word of encouragement, you should feel blessed while performing services for God's glory.

Ask yourself, "What service has God impressed upon me to give?" If you know what it is, then ask yourself, "Am I happy when I perform this service for God?" If you have not received unction from God then your prayer should be, "Lord, I want to be blessed by providing services for You. Lead me to what You want me to do." I guarantee that if you are sincere about doing God's work, He will direct you in the area of service that is tailored for you. He will also lead you to pray as you give yourself to spiritual service for Him.

Now, it's your time to be blessed for service. So go ahead; take that first step. Don't be afraid! Why not approach God in prayer right now? He is waiting to make you blessed (happy).

MY PRAYER FOR YOU

Lord, send Your Holy Spirit now and minister to the readers of this book. Reveal Your divine assignments to them. Tell them what to do; show them how to do it. Bless them as they follow Your instructions. As they pray to You give them keen spiritual ears to hear what You are saying. Remove all dullness from their hearing, so they can hear Your directions clearly. Let them move forward in You rendering service for Your honor and glory. Let them be blessed beyond measure. In Jesus' name, I pray. Amen!

CHAPTER 4

APPOINTED TO BE ANOINTED

The Spirit of the Lord God is upon me; because the Lord hath anointed me to preach good tidings unto the meek; he hath sent me to bind up the broken-hearted, to proclaim liberty to the captives, and the opening of the prison to them that are bound; To proclaim the acceptable year of the Lord, and the day of vengeance of our God; to comfort all that mourn; To appoint unto them that mourn in Zion, to give unto them beauty for ashes, the oil of joy for mourning, the garment of praise for the spirit of heaviness; that they might be called trees of righteousness, the planting of the Lord that he might be glorified. (Isaiah 61:1-3)

What a powerful scripture that lets you know what you are appointed and anointed to do.

To appoint is to select or designate, to fill an office or position. It also means to furnish or equip. God has selected and equipped you and me to reach souls with the gospel of salvation. Additionally, He has appointed you to receive an anointing from Him when you pray.

To anoint is to authorize or set apart a person for a particular work or service. To be anointed is to be empowered by the Spirit of God to perform special tasks that require the power of God to flow from Him through you.

To have the anointing of God is a privilege. To be recognized as God's anointed is favor. There is always a responsibility in having and keeping the anointing of God in your life. The best way to do that is through prayer.

When you are equipped with God's anointing, you have access to an invaluable treasure of authority and empowerment. As you pray, the Holy Spirit intercedes for you. While this is taking place, He (the Holy Spirit) seals that anointing within you so you can do ministry for God.

When you have the anointing of God at work in your life, the manifestation of His power is revealed in various ways, especially through the gifts of the Spirit (Read 1 Corinthians 12:1-11).

Please understand that it takes consistency in prayer and building your relationship with God for His anointing to empower you to deal with any task at hand. Through prayer, you keep yourself reserved for use by the Master. Why do I say that? Well, when you pray, you open up yourself for God to reveal your good attributes and characteristics, as well as your shortcomings. That way, you can correct those areas that need fixing and allow God to appoint and empower you as a vessel of honor He can minister through.

As you are saturated with the anointing of God through prayer, you become a willing servant desiring to move when God says to move, speak what God says to speak, and do what He wants you to do.

THE OVERFLOW

As you pray to be filled with the anointing of God, tell Him, "Lord, give me an overflow of Your Spirit." You see, when you have an overflow of God's Spirit, you can truly experience the power of God enabling you to move freely in Him.

Right now, I want you to take an empty glass and set it in front of you. If I were to ask you how you would remove the air from that glass, what would your response be? Would you say, "Remove it with a pump"? Well, if you attempt to do that, you might shatter the glass. Maybe you would say, "Turn the glass over." That would just trap the air inside the glass.

Allow God to appoint and empower you

I want you to pour water into the glass and fill it up to capacity. What happened to the air? Yes, you're right! It is now gone and replaced with a refreshing substance.

Think of yourself as the glass. Think of the air as stagnation, emptiness, excuses, discouragement, doubt, and even sin. If you want the anointing of God to work abundantly in you, you must first ask God to cleanse you from all the ugliness of sin, emptiness, doubt, discouragement, stagnation, and excuses. Ask Him to fill you up with His Holy Spirit.

Now, if you were to pour one more drop of water in the glass, what would happen? It would overflow. That is what you want – an overflow of God's Spirit, so you can be equipped with His anointing.

When you experience the outpour and in-filling of the Holy Spirit, your lifestyle, attitude, and outlook on life will change. Consequently, your awareness of the anointing of God is enhanced and expanded. To get to this point, you must learn to persevere in prayer daily, along with fasting, studying, and meditating on God's Word.

The overflow of God's Spirit fulfills your spiritual desires, provides inspiration, and encourages your soul. It also helps you to gain the power and authority Luke speaks about.

> Behold I give unto you power to tread on serpents and scorpions, and over all the power of the enemy; and nothing shall by any means hurt you. (Luke 10:19)

Please understand that through the power of prayer, you can win the battle against the devil, gain victory in any circumstance and have access to the anointing of God in abundance.

FASTING AND PRAYER

In 1996, the Spirit of the Lord spoke to me and instructed me to go on a 10-day consecration of water only – no food. Of course, I told the Lord I couldn't do it because I would pass out. But God kept urging me to go on the 10-day water-only fast. So I finally said yes to Him. During this time, I was going through some trials. I was so tired and frustrated with the attacks of the devil that I was totally miserable. I prayed and asked God to strengthen me for the task. I asked Him not to let the devil gain any ground with his weapons and arrows of adversity.

I yielded to the commands and instructions of God. I also gave myself over to fasting and prayer. As a result, I found myself with an attitude of power and authority over any and everything the devil tried to bring my way. You see, a few months before the fast, I was ready to leave everything and everybody – except God. I felt within myself if I left and started all over somewhere else, I would be alright. However, I soon realized that thought pattern was from the devil. You can never run away from your trials; you have to face the music and deal with the trials.

As I began my journey of fasting and prayer, the first three days were hard but not unbearable. However, on the fourth day, I felt as if I would not make it. My head throbbed; my stomach cramped, and I felt so weak in my body that I could hardly stand. In that condition, all I wanted was relief. I had a job to go to, as well as a house and family to take care of. It was painful. However, my prayers intensified because I was determined to make it to the end of the 10 days. I recall the Lord instructing me to get a glass of warm water and His Word. He told me to sip the water as I read His Word. Oh my, what a total release I gained from the agony of the flesh.

LORD, BREATHE ON ME

During this particular consecration, I was asked to preach the Sunday morning sermon at my local church for the Women's

Day Service. I sought God each day about what I was to give to His people. On the fifth day of the fast, two days before I had to deliver my sermon, God gave me the word He wanted me to deliver. My scripture text was found in Ezekiel 37. God gave me this subject: "Lord, Breathe on Me." As I meditated on His Word and put together a few notes, I got very excited about how God had saturated me with His anointing to prepare the sermon, as well as deliver it.

On the seventh day of the fast, which was the Sunday, I began my discourse on "Lord, Breathe on Me." The overwhelming anointing of God convinced me I could conquer anything that came my way. I knew as long as God was breathing on me, I would have power. I would have strength and victory. I experienced such exponential growth spiritually that I will never forget that period of my life. I grew closer to God during those 10 days, and I didn't regress after the fast was over. I had a keen awareness of the increase of God's power in me, which went beyond anything I could have imagined His power could do in my life.

People came to me after the service asking me what happened because they had never seen such authority and boldness. My response was that it was God, and all the glory and honor belong to Him. To this day, I thank God for the souls who were saved, delivered, and set free on that Sunday morning. I thank Him for opening my spiritual eyes to see that to have the power and anointing of God at work in my life, I had to make sacrifices and dedicate myself to prayer and fasting.

The next three days were a breeze. I felt as if I had eaten a fresh meal each day. In those ten days, God gave me lots of insight about Him and how He works. It enriched my life to the point where even today, I value fasting and consecrating myself before the Lord. A real benefit was learning to keep my focus on God and not on my situation. Was the trial still going on? Yes, it was, but my focus was on the problem solver, not on the problem.

Right now, ask God, "Lord, what am I appointed and anointed to do?" Ask God for His instructions; follow them to the letter, and watch the change occur in you spiritually.

MY PRAYER FOR YOU

Gracious and heavenly Father, I pray for Your servants whom You have appointed and anointed to do battle for Your kingdom. Give them insight into the importance of prayer and fasting. May they recognize that to have Your power, it will take consecrating their lives to You. Right now, breathe Your anointing on them, and let it saturate them from the crown of their heads to the soles of their feet. Lord, empower them with Your authority, courage, wisdom, and strength. Allow them to experience spiritual growth and an awakening of Your anointing as they give of themselves totally to You. I ask all of this in the name of your Son, Jesus. Amen!

CHAPTER 5

WALK IN YOUR DELIVERANCE

This I say then, walk in the Spirit and ye shall not fulfill the lust of the flesh. (Galatians 5:16)

See then that ye walk circumspectly, not as fools, but as wise, redeeming the time, because the days are evil. (Ephesians 5:15-16)

Let us begin with an affirmation. Repeat this statement: "I am delivered, and I will stay delivered by walking in my deliverance through prayer."

Now that you have affirmed you are delivered, let's look at what it means to walk in your deliverance. You must first understand that as you journey in this life, the enemy will try to bind, tempt, hinder and even ensnare you with the cares of this life. When this happens, don't stay or wallow in your struggles. Instead, call upon God the Father to help and deliver you. Many times, we allow the devil to keep us trapped in sin, hopelessness, depression, and self-pity – to name a few – which creates strongholds that hinder spiritual growth. When there is stagnation, there is always a need for deliverance.

Deliverance is the action of being set free. When people are in bondage, they become hopeless. If you are in that condition right now, don't give up! Just keep reading because your complete deliverance is nigh. What you need at this moment is a breakthrough prayer! What is a breakthrough prayer? It is a prayer so intense that your focus is on nothing more than being free from the feelings of entrapment. You are imprisoned in your mind, as well as your spirit-man. Whenever you get to this point, deliverance from the hands of Satan is paramount.

I recall being bound by the spirit of depression. This spirit had me not loving myself, which created the feeling that no one else did either. I felt like a lost cause. I put on a very good façade, but on the inside, there was a war going on. I cried and stayed by myself often. At times, I responded to people with a defensive attitude. I would mentally put myself down because I didn't like the way I looked or felt. Can you imagine not liking yourself? Well, that is the way I was.

I faced myself every day and did not like me. I felt like I was nothing. During this time, I was married, and this spirit of depression made me think my husband didn't love me. No matter how much he told me he loved me, I could not accept or believe it. I was bound by this spirit, and I wanted to be set free. Yes, I was a child of God, but I was in an awful state. I didn't know how to be set free and went as far as seeing a psychiatrist, but that didn't help either.

THE BREAKING POINT

The breaking point for me was when I went to my beautician. She asked me what I had done to my hair because I had a bald spot the size of a quarter at the top of my head. When she showed me, I started to cry. I made an appointment to see a dermatologist. The dermatologist told me I had a condition called "alopecia," which is a nervous condition that generates hair loss. I had to have several treatments, which consisted of injections in my scalp to stimulate the hair follicles.

I remember going home after my appointment, lying on the floor in my bedroom and praying a breakthrough prayer. I told God that I needed peace in my mind and spirit. I told Him I wanted deliverance from depression and misery. I also asked Him if He didn't deliver me, how I could tell others He would deliver them. That day, I screamed, cried, hit the floor, and rolled back and forth. Finally, I composed myself and said, "Lord, I'm going to sleep, but when I wake up, I want to be free. I want to have peace in my mind and spirit." When I awoke, I heard the Spirit of God say to me, "How can you not like what I created?"

> *What you need at this moment is a breakthrough prayer!*

The spirit of depression will make you act and think inappropriately. So when God made that statement to me again, I began to talk about what I didn't like about myself and how I felt even as a child. The Lord listened to me and again, He asked, "How can you not like what I created?" Then He instructed me to look in the mirror, tell myself I was beautiful and that I loved me for me. My response to God was that I couldn't do that because I didn't feel that way. However, He was relentless. He sent me to look in the mirror again to repeat the same words. So with tears in my eyes, I went to the mirror. I stood there staring at myself thinking about the question and the instructions. Finally, I found the courage to say, "I'm beautiful, and I love me for me."

The Lord said to me, "Say it again," so I did. He told me to repeat those words until I felt them on the inside. I did just that, and those feelings of unhappiness, dislike, and despair left. I was overshadowed by an overwhelming spirit of peace and joy. That moment marked the beginning of my deliverance walk, which continues to this day. As a matter of fact, one morning while my husband and I were preparing for worship service, I looked in the mirror, and I said out loud, "Girl, you're beautiful!" Then I winked at myself. My husband looked at me and asked, "Where did that come from?" He had never heard me make a statement like that about myself. He said, "I already knew you were beautiful." We laughed.

AFFIRMATIONS

My walk in deliverance did not stop with that experience. I developed affirmations that I still say. And yes, I still say I'm beautiful even if no one else thinks so. I am secure in knowing that I was fearfully and wonderfully made by God (Psalm 139:14). God beautifies the meek with salvation (Psalm 149:4). I enjoy creating affirmations that will address any area of my life. Here are some of my affirmations that have helped me stay focused on my deliverance walk:

- I will not fail in my efforts. I will succeed according to God's divine plan, purpose, and will for my life. In Jesus' name
- That which I speak will come to pass. I will not allow doubt in my mind to last. I believe in God's promises because He is faithful to His Word. I will totally trust Him and not be detoured
- God has given me the power to stand and go through the test. I know that I'll make it because God is on my side
- There is nothing that God will refuse to do for me if I keep my focus on Him and totally trust Him

Do you know in what area of your life you need deliverance? Don't hide it or try to sweep it under the carpet. Confess it to God and ask Him for forgiveness and deliverance. When you receive your instructions from Him, follow them. Don't stop performing that task until you get a total breakthrough on the inside. Keep the following scripture in mind as you walk in your deliverance.

If the Son therefore shall make you free, ye shall be free indeed. (John 8:36)

When you become free, keep telling yourself you are free because that's what is written in God's Word. What does the Word of God say?

Death and life are in the power of the tongue; and they that love it shall eat the fruit thereof. (Proverbs 18:21)

If you want to continue to eat the fruit of life, you must speak life.

DELIVERANCE THROUGH PRAYER

The word "deliverance" can be used as an acronym you can refer to as you walk in your deliverance through prayer. When you look at each phrase, develop a prayer asking God to help you to grow spiritually in each area:

- **D**edicate yourself to righteous living
- **E**levate your thoughts toward God
- **L**earn to trust God for everything
- **I**nvest time in communicating with God
- **V**alue yourself as a child of God
- **E**njoy being in a relationship with God
- **R**esist Satan daily
- **A**nticipate a miracle from God
- **N**ever give in to Satan's tactics
- **C**ommit yourself to the service of God
- **E**xpect only positive results

Deliverance comes through commitment to prayer and daily meditation on God's Word. You must learn to encourage yourself. Tell yourself you can make it. Don't allow the accuser of the brethren (Satan) to make you feel there is no hope.

> I can do all things through Christ which strengtheneth me. (Philippians 4:13)

I encourage you to continue affirming that you can make it. Always remember God will never ever fail you. Do you see that word "ever" in "never"? You have the power to be free and stay free.

YOUR SPIRITUAL WALK

The word "walk" in this context refers to the activities performed in your life. The activities you do in your Christian walk should be filled with purpose, need, certainty, and a positive outlook. Naturally, walking as an exercise strengthens you, builds your cardiovascular system and produces a metabolic flow of energy. When you make an effort spiritually to walk in your deliverance, you will begin to build your spiritual muscles that will help you combat the enemy.

When walking in your deliverance, you must believe it; speak it; embrace it; act upon it; practice it and more importantly, master it. Remember these are positive actions, and the transforming power of the Holy Spirit will help you overcome any of life's challenges.

Keep in mind that your walk in your deliverance is not a secret; it's a system of God. You can master this system by praying to Him daily asking for guidance. God is the architect, and His Word is the blueprint. Your life will be built on a sure foundation as you put God first in all you do. Walk in His power of deliverance.

MY PRAYER FOR YOU

Gracious Father, the One who knows all things and can perform anything, touch those who are struggling against bondage and strongholds and recognize their need for deliverance. Send Your spiritual power of deliverance now. Teach them how to walk in their deliverance by communicating with You. Lord, let them realize that every obstacle can present an opportunity to improve their condition when they stand firm on the promises outlined in Your Word. God, give them the security to know You will always be there for them. You will never leave or forsake them. Overshadow them now with the power of Your love and provide the confirmation of the Holy Spirit as He ministers to them, instructing and directing them to lives of freedom. All of these blessings I ask in the name of Your precious Son, Jesus. Amen.

CHAPTER 6

SEVEN KEYS TO SUCCESS GOD'S WAY

This book of the law shall not depart out of thy mouth; but thou shalt meditate therein day and night, that thou mayest observe to do according to all that is written therein; for then thou shalt make thy way prosperous, and then thou shalt have good success. (Joshua 1:8)

*T*he most important element in achieving a favorable outcome in your Christian walk is your commitment to God, along with applying the 3-P's approach – Pray, Pray, Pray. This is one of the keys to becoming successful God's way. When you apply the 3-P's approach, it will produce Praise, Perseverance, and Power. I think those are some good attributes to have.

In life, there are many successes and also things you may consider failures. Most of the time when you look at success, you look at your financial status or position in life career-wise, as well as in the church arena.

When a person is successful, the question is always asked, "What is the secret to your success?" You never hear anyone asking, "What is the secret to your failure?" This is because no one aspires to fail. Everyone wants to succeed; therefore, they want to know, "How do I open that secret door to success?"

There is a familiar passage of Scripture that I want to use to point out some essential keys to success in this story. It's the story of Joshua leading the Israelites to possess the land God promised them. In Joshua Chapter 5, Joshua had an encounter with God similar to the one Moses had. In Chapter 6, God speaks to Joshua informing him that he would conquer Jericho. However, some things had to be done first.

THE ESSENTIAL KEYS

The first essential key is that Joshua had a relationship with God. When you have a relationship with God, you can hear the instructions He gives clearly. Joshua listened intently to God's directions and then he obeyed the voice of God.

The second key is that Joshua did not deviate from what God told him to do. Rather, he followed the instructions to the letter. One of the instructions given was where to place the Ark of the Covenant, which represented the presence of God.

The next essential key is to keep God in the midst of all you do. Remember this Scripture:

> Trust in the Lord with all thine heart and lean not unto
> thine own understanding. In all thy ways acknowledge
> Him and He shall direct thy path. (Proverbs 3:5-6)

When you trust God and acknowledge Him in all things, you keep Him at the forefront in everything you do.

Joshua and the Israelites put together the plan of action directed by God. The essential key here is that they put action to their faith that what God had already predicted would happen. When you pray, listen, obey, put forth the effort and diligently perform what God says, God's divine order of plans will fall in line just as He promises.

DECENTLY AND IN ORDER

Joshua and the Israelites did exactly what God asked them to do and that was to march. But they had to march a certain way. There was order in what they did. Strength and courage were included in that order. Doing all things decently and in order is an essential key because God is a God of order.

Keep in mind that success requires sacrifices.

Let's look at the order. There were armed guards in front of the procession. Next in line were seven priests carrying seven trumpets and then the Ark of the Covenant. Finally, there were armed guards at the rear of the Ark of the Covenant.

The children of Israel had to march silently around the walls of Jericho for six days straight, and on the seventh day, they had to march around Jericho seven times. The trumpets of ram's horns produced a loud, far-sounding tone to give signals rather than music. This sound summoned them to prepare for battle. Everything had to be in order for the plan to work. That is why it is important for you to know what God wants you to say, how He wants you to say it, what you are to do and how He wants you to do it.

SEVEN – THE NUMBER OF PERFECTION

The number seven is special. If you notice, God said to have seven priests with seven trumpets march around the Jericho walls seven times on the seventh day. The number seven goes all the way back to creation. The final day of the creation week gave the number seven special significance. It symbolized completeness or perfection. So God used seven because He knew on the seventh day, Jericho would be totally destroyed. The only people saved were Rahab and her family because she hid the Israelite spies when they went to observe the land. Joshua and the Israelites' obedience ultimately resulted in victory for them.

Doing all things God's way and not your way will get you the victory. You will have great success. Keep in mind that success requires sacrifices. You may have to make some sacrifices, but it is worth it when it is done God's way. Malachi 3:6 says that God will not change. So if He did it for Joshua, He will do it for you.

Here are seven keys to use that will ensure your success in all that you do when you do it God's way:

KEY #1 – A RELATIONSHIP WITH GOD

This includes communicating with Him (prayer), meditating on His Word (instruction manual), consecration to Him (fasting), reverencing and worshiping Him (submission), listening to His instructions and then obeying them. In your relationship with God, you put Him first in everything. You try to live a life above reproach. You determine within yourself to do His will and follow His way. God knows what is best for you anyway – and that includes success.

> Seek ye first the kingdom of God and His righteousness and all of these things shall be added unto you.
> (Matthew 6:33)

KEY #2 – FAITH

Obviously, you must believe in God. However, you must also believe in yourself and that you can do all things through Christ who strengthens you (Philippians 4:13). Learn to put action to your faith like Joshua did. Faith in action brings about God's divine results. Trust God for your successes in life because He is in control of everything. God will hold you up, and He will stand under the pressures of your adversities. Then, He wants you to lean on Him and don't doubt. That is faith in action.

KEY #3 – PERSEVERANCE

To persevere is to adhere to a course of action, belief or purpose without giving way, steadfastness, persistence. Perseverance entails having the patience to withstand difficulties or resistance. In this life, every day will not be sunshine; therefore, pressing toward your mark and goals spiritually and naturally will take perseverance. Below are two scriptures that let you know perseverance is a key God wants you to have as you travel toward your goal of success:

> Therefore, my beloved brethren, be ye steadfast unmovable, always abounding in the work of the Lord, forasmuch as ye know that your labor is not in vain in the Lord. (1 Corinthians 15:58)

> And let us not be weary in well doing; for in due season, we shall reap; If we faint not. (Galatians 6:9)

KEY #4 – COMMITMENT AND CONSISTENCY

Commitment is responsibility and determination. Consistency is constant performance, steady effort. It is faithfulness in reaching your goals. Success God's way says, "I will take responsibility for my actions. No matter what comes my way, I will remain faithful to God and His divine goals for my life."

> Delight thyself also in the Lord; and He shall give thee the desires of thine heart. Commit thy way unto the Lord; trust also in Him and He shall bring it to pass. (Psalm 37:4-5)

Jesus said:

> Be thou faithful unto death and I will give thee a crown of life. (Revelation 2:10b)

Even if you have to go through trials, tribulations, afflictions, complications, and more to receive your reward, making that commitment to be consistent will allow you to be successful.

KEY #5 – POSITIVE ATTITUDE

Having confidence in God will generate confidence in yourself.

> For the Lord shall be thy confidence, and shall keep thy foot from being taken. (Proverbs 3:26)

Oh, what an awesome promise! Think positive; speak positive; look positive; act positive, and be around positive people. Watch the positive results that will occur in your life. Always remember that a negative attitude can hinder your progress.

KEY #6 – STAY FOCUSED ON GOD

Don't let the devil take you off track. When adversities or complications arise, don't panic. Don't get sidetracked by focusing on your situation. Instead, look to Jesus who is the problem solver.

> Seek ye the Lord while He may be found, call ye upon Him while He is near. (Isaiah 55:6)

When you are searching for something, you focus on it totally.

KEY #7 – BE STRONG AND COURAGEOUS

Strength exhibits the power to sustain or resist attacks. To be strong is to have a firmness of will, character, mind or purpose, which is moral courage or power. Courage is the state or quality of mind or spirit that enables one to face a situation with confidence. That's why God told Joshua to be strong and courageous. He knew the end result would be prosperity and success. We must learn to take on the same attributes.

Success God's way is designed by Him and Him only. Rehearse those seven keys to success God's way, and your way will be prosperous; you will have good success.

MY PRAYER FOR YOU

Gracious and eternal Savior, I pray for the success of all those reading this prayer. Make them successful spiritually, mentally, physically, and financially. Teach them how to put You first in all they do. Give them the courage to obey Your commands without reservation. Direct them on how to put action to their faith. Lord, continue to remind them of Your omnipotence and that all power belongs to You. Give them strength to be still and know that You are God. Allow them to experience Your divine miracles at work in every area of their lives. I speak Your blessings of courage, prosperity, and success upon each one. It shall be done according to Your promises. In Jesus' name, I pray. Amen.

CHAPTER 7

SPIRITUAL WEALTH IN THE SECRET PLACE

He that dwelleth in the secret place of the Most High shall abide under the shadow of the Almighty. (Psalm 91:1)

*H*ave you ever sat and daydreamed of being wealthy? You know how you play out an entire scenario in your mind. You imagine all the things you would purchase. You think about all of the people you would help and what charities you would give donations to. You daydream about the beachfront home, luxury cars, designer clothes, lavish trips, and sparkling jewelry. You go on and on. It feels very real and satisfying until suddenly, you snap into reality. You recognize that you are not wealthy, at least, not monetarily.

Have you ever daydreamed about being spiritually wealthy? Have you considered the number of souls you want to bring to the kingdom or how many lives you can touch with a word of encouragement? When I speak about spiritual wealth, I am not only talking about laying hands on others to see them get healed, delivered, and set free but also laying hands on yourself and receiving the same results.

When you are spiritually wealthy, you are richly supplied in abundance. Spiritual wealth allows you to speak to the mountains and obstacles in your life and command them to go. Those mountains and negative situations have to obey your command.

How do you get this spiritual wealth? You obtain it in the secret place of God. How do you get to the secret place of God? You get to this secret place as you avail yourself to prayer continually and dwell there.

Spiritual wealth is a treasure that will not be affected by moths, rust or thieves (Matthew 6:19-20). When you are in the secret place of God, you enter a zone beyond ordinary understanding that is only known or shared by the one who has initiated the entrance. Once you submit yourself totally to God, and you are not concerned about what your flesh thinks or feels, you have made a step into God's secret place. Nothing can harm you there.

> The name of the Lord is a strong tower; the righteous runneth into it, and is safe. (Proverbs 18:10)

The name of the Lord protects us and lifts us out of the reach of the devil when we are in God's secret place. To enter the secret place of God, you must first reach the key that will unlock the heart of God.

THE LANDMARKS

You will make some stops along the way, and each stop will be your landmark with instructions for you to follow. A landmark is a guide, marker or turning point. When you do not follow the instructions at these landmarks, there will be danger ahead.

The journey is your Christian walk with God. The landmarks are instructions given by God, which are found in the Word of God. They will be needed to reach that secret place in God.

You are traveling on your journey, and you have reached your first landmark. This landmark is the MIND/BODY and HEART/SOUL. It says that at all times, you

How do you get to the secret place of God?

must ensure your heart and soul are right with God. Furthermore, you must keep your mind and body in line and under the subjection of the Spirit of God.

Take a look at your spiritual map to be sure you are on the correct path to your destination. Your spiritual map is the Word of God, which says the following about the mind, body, heart, and soul:

> Keep thy heart with all diligence; for out of it are the issues of life. (Proverbs 4:23)

> Behold, all souls are mine as the soul of the father, so also the soul of the son is mine; the soul that sinneth it shall die. (Ezekiel 18:4)

> And be not conformed to this world; but be ye trans-
> formed by the renewing of your mind, that ye may
> prove what is that good, and acceptable, and perfect,
> will of God. (Romans 12:2)

> What? Know ye not that your body is the temple of
> the Holy Ghost which is in you, which ye have of God
> and ye are not your own? For ye are bought with a price
> therefore glorify God in your body and in your spirit,
> which are God's. (1 Corinthians 6:19-20)

As you go a little further on your Christian journey, you will
reach your second landmark. This landmark is STUDY & MEDI-
TATION. This is where you learn to diligently study and meditate on God's Word. You should have a desire to study God's
Word just like you would study to get a degree or for an examination to enhance the promotional opportunities on your job.

The Word of God is not only your spiritual roadmap, but it
is also your insurance policy. Naturally, as long as your insurance premiums are paid, you are covered. Spiritually, you keep
coverage as long as you are obeying the truth of God's Word.
However, to know what your coverage is, you must study
your policy.

Finally, you reach your last landmark, PRAYER & FASTING.
Seeking to know God daily through prayer keeps your soul
tuned in and your spiritual communication line open. Fasting
weakens the flesh but builds up the spiritual muscles of the
inner spirit-man.

> Jesus said unto them, Because of your unbelief: for ver-
> ily I say unto you, if ye have faith as a grain of mustard

seed, ye shall say unto this mountain, remove hence to yonder place; and it shall remove; and nothing shall be impossible unto you. Howbeit this kind goeth not out but by prayer and fasting. (Matthew 17:20-21)

In Luke 18:1, it tells us that men (mankind) should always pray and not faint. Prayer and fasting will keep us from fainting when adversity rears its ugly head.

You have received instructions at each landmark and must continue to water, clean, and fertilize these areas. You cannot allow them to lie dormant. Naturally speaking, when you see a famous landmark that is dirty and run down you wonder, "Why didn't someone do something about it to make it presentable?" The same is true with your Christian walk. You must be presentable to God at all times, especially if you want to enter His secret place.

BEWARE OF PITFALLS

Your journey is not over; you must reach that secret place in God. The devil does not want you to reach your destination; his job is to place some pitfalls in your way during your journey. Sadly, some of these pitfalls are the areas that keep a lot of people from reaching and even staying in the secret place of God. The following are some of the pitfalls the devil places in your way:

- Hurts, pains, disappointments – These can generate a spirit of depression. When you carry this stuff, it will eventually produce other issues e.g. self-destruction
- Unforgiveness – This generates bitterness, holding of grudges, hatred, and physical sickness

- Self-righteousness – This type of mannerism causes people to isolate themselves. It is like being on an island all alone
- Doubt – This delays and hinders the miracle-working power and blessings of God that He has carefully prepared for you
- Hypocrisy – This is a characteristic of people who pretend to be something they are not
- Evil/Wickedness – People who are evil and have the spirit of wickedness are vicious, mischievous, obnoxious, and offensive. They are morally distasteful

These are just a few pitfalls the devil uses to try to hinder you from reaching the secret place in God. Galatians 5:19-21 gives a list of the works of the flesh. These are even more pitfalls the devil uses to keep you from reaching a higher spiritual level in God.

To avoid these devil-designed pitfalls, you must follow the instructions in your combat manual, the Bible.

> Watch and pray, that ye enter not into temptation; the spirit indeed is willing, but the flesh is weak.
> (Matthew 26:41)

You have to be on continuous alert for the traps of Satan. Do this by fasting and praying.

UNLOCKING THE HEART OF GOD

Once you have reached the landmarks, read your instructions, maintained the landmarks, as well as avoided all the pitfalls of

Satan, you have reached the key. The key is praise and worship. You praise God for all that He does, but you worship Him for who He is. Praise and worship are the keys that let you empty yourself before God and submit everything to Him. When you do this, you unlock the heart of God and enter His secret place.

In God's secret place, you desire, hunger, and want whatever God wants; nothing else matters but to please Him. You find peace, joy, and happiness in His secret place. Whatever concerns or questions you may have, you will find the answers there.

I thought about Daniel in the Bible when a decree went out saying anyone caught praying to God would be thrown into the lion's den. Daniel had reached that secret place in God because in spite of the known consequences, Daniel kept his window open for all to see him do what he did daily – pray. He was determined to pray no matter what happened.

Daniel was placed in the lion's den. However, because he dwelled in the secret place of God, the lions could not touch him. Daniel is just one of many examples in the Bible who were victorious.

You will find spiritual wealth and comfort when you pray. It is like putting money in your bank, the more you put in, the more your interest will be and the wealthier you will become.

A TRIAL OF MY FAITH

There was a time in my life when I needed to make sure I was in the secret place of God. In 1989, I had a pituitary tumor that caused my body not to function properly in certain areas.

After speaking with doctors and hearing my alternatives, I prayed and asked God, "What should I do?" I chose to have the tumor surgically removed.

With any surgery, the doctors will always tell you about the probable mishaps that could occur. They told me I could die. I could become blind or be in a vegetative state if something unfortunate happened during the surgery. They told me that the surgery would take about six hours to perform. Needless to say, I was nervous. Although I had the best surgeon there was to perform this type of surgery, I still had reservations about the whole procedure.

I remember contacting a friend of mine to meet me at the church where we could touch and agree in prayer regarding the surgery. We prayed on a Friday, a couple of weeks before my surgery. I remember telling God that I did not want to be unconscious for more than four hours. I told God that I did not want the extensive cutting the doctor described. I prayed for the doctors and the nurses that God would guide their hands, and He would not allow anything to go wrong.

There were many tests that I had to take and different specialists that I had to see before the actual surgery. The last specialist I went to checked my nose structure to see how extensive the cutting would be. Well, after my examination, she came to me and said it was rare to see the type of nose structure I had and that the extensive cutting would not be necessary. She informed me that the doctors would be able to go through my nose to get to the pituitary and remove the tumor. Of course, I was ecstatic about that finding. And yes, I did praise God for the answer to that portion of my prayer.

The night before surgery, my husband sat down with the surgeon to provide a list of instructions. He asked the surgeon to get a good night's rest and eat a good breakfast before coming to perform the surgery. Although we laugh about it now, at that time, it was a very serious situation.

On February 23, 1990, I arrived at the hospital very early and was taken into the pre-op room to undergo preparation for the operation. During this time, I was praying and asking God to be with me and to keep me calm and relaxed. At that moment, the anesthesiologist came in and proceeded to inform me that there was one thing the doctor forgot to tell me; they were going to have to drain the fluid off my brain. This consisted of a needle being inserted into my spine along with a tube to drain the fluid. After he told me that, fear literally gripped me. But then the Spirit of the Lord spoke these words to me, "I have not given you the spirit of fear, but of love, and of power and of a sound mind. It will be alright." I lay there thanking God for His presence with me.

When I entered the operating room, I told the Lord that I wanted Him to be with me and that if it was my time to go, I wanted to be ready. Of course, I asked God to cleanse me and to forgive all the wrongdoings in my life from birth until that point. Then a nurse came over to me, bent down and said, "You are a Christian, aren't you?" I responded, "Yes, I am." She then told me that God had placed an angel in the operating room with me, and I did not have to worry about anything. I could not help but let the tears flow because God wanted me to know He was there. I never saw that nurse again.

My surgery was successful, and I was only unconscious for four hours just as I had prayed. During that time, and even throughout my recovery, I fell deeper and deeper in love with prayer. Communicating with God, hearing from Him, and experiencing the manifestation of His miracle-working power are awesome.

If you really want to get to that secret place of God and dwell there, you must learn to touch God through prayer. You will discover many jewels of wisdom and knowledge, and you will experience many miracles to treasure for the rest of your days. Why not get on your knees right now and begin your journey to the secret place of God? When you get there, stay there and receive a continuous flow of God's blessings, anointing, and deliverance.

MY PRAYER FOR YOU

Father God, in the name of Your Son, Jesus, please teach each one how to enter Your secret place. Give all the readers a hunger and thirst to seek Your face and to touch You as they pray. Bless them to become spiritually wealthy and to know You beyond their highest dreams. Keep them in tune with Your Spirit as they experience You in a real way. Open their understanding of Your inner workings in their lives. Help them to stay focused by rehearsing the promises of Your Word in their minds and hearts. Lead and guide them into all truth and give them continuous peace. All of these many blessings I ask in Jesus' name. It shall be done. Amen.

CHAPTER 8

ACTION PLAN

Therefore I say unto you, What things soever ye desire, when ye pray, believe that ye receive them, and ye shall have them. (Mark 11:24)

And this is the confidence that we have in him, that, if we ask any thing according to his will, he heareth us: And if we know that he hear us, whatsoever we ask, we know that we have the petitions that we desired of him. (1 John 5:14-15)

*N*ow it is time to take action to become blessed, anointed, and delivered through prayer. As you develop your relationship with God in prayer, you will find that prayer will become your safety zone. I encourage you to walk in P.A.R (pray, accept, receive) excellence. The word "par" means equality of value; equally balanced. You can only have a balanced life when you put prayer into practice daily. Each day, your prayer should be,

"Lord, anoint me to pray; appoint me to accept and empower me to receive all that You have for me."

When you pray, you build effectiveness in your prayer life, which, in turn, generates the power to heal, deliver and live in a state of freedom. When you pray, you are taking your daily prescription, the necessary vitamins that will ward off hurt, pain, problems, and disappointments. Taking the prayer prescription is a preventive measure that will keep situations from becoming worse spiritually, emotionally, and naturally. This prayer prescription is a sedative that gives peace in the midst of a storm. Will adverse situations occur in your life? Of course! However, your responses to them will change when you pray.

Prayer is the greatest privilege of your Christian life and the most revolutionary source of power known to mankind. Always remember that God dwells where the spirit of prayer resides.

SPIRITUAL FOOD FOR THOUGHT

- Learn to keep a passion to pray
- Be committed to believing God's promises outlined in His Word
- Be receptive without hesitation to receive God's favor in your life while being consistent in prayer

The best commitment you could ever make is to communicate with God in prayer. Try approaching God in prayer for 15 minutes a day uninterrupted for the next three weeks and watch what happens in your life. If you want happiness, pray. If you want joy, pray. If you want peace, pray. If you want to be healed, pray. If you want to lack nothing, pray. If you want to be blessed, pray. If you want God's anointing, pray. If you want God's power, pray. If you want God's deliverance, pray. If you want to be successful, pray. If you want spiritual wealth, pray.

Don't forget the 3-P's approach to anything you come across in this life – PRAY, PRAY, PRAY. Remember that prayer is the key to unlock the door of God's heart, and it will change you.

I thank you for taking the time to read this book. I pray you have been encouraged to become BAD and stay BAD through the power of prayer.

Taking the prayer prescription is a preventive measure.

MY PRAYER FOR YOU

Dear heavenly Father, thank You for being the King of kings, Lord of lords and the caretaker of this soul. Thank You for those reading this prayer right now. Teach them the art of prayer. Bless them to become prayer vessels for You. Pour Your wisdom, power, anointing, love, understanding, and resilience into their hearts as they begin their journeys in prayer. Lord, allow each and every person who moves forward in developing their prayer life with You to be enriched, empowered, enlightened, blessed, and successful beyond what they could even imagine. I declare and decree these things to occur in their lives. In Jesus' name, I pray. Amen!

ABOUT THE AUTHOR

*L*ady Phyllis Thomas is the First Lady of Showers of Blessings Church located in Sacramento, California. A licensed missionary, her objective is to be a supporter, encourager, motivator, and intercessor.

Lady Thomas serves in various capacities in the local church. She is a Sunday School Teacher, Christian Education Department Instructor, President of the Evangelist/Missionary Circle, Women's Department President/Advisor, President of the Young Women of Purpose Group, Prayer Warrior, and Spiritual Guidance Advisor. Lady Thomas is also a Volunteer Chaplain for the Sacramento County Jail Facilities.

A recipient of a G.O.D degree (God-given Opportunity to Deliver His Word), she has been inducted into the C.B.G. (Chosen by God) Club for a lifetime of service. She reminds herself of the importance of prayer with the initials of her name PNT: **P**ray **N**ow **T**hink **L**ater.

Lady Thomas is a real estate professional by trade. She has also been employed with the State of California as an Associate Analyst and is now retired. Although she wears many hats, she encourages herself with this scripture that says, "I can do all things through Christ that strengthens me" (Philippians 4:13).

Lady Thomas resides in Elk Grove, California with her husband of over 37 years, Dr. Darnell Thomas, pastor of the Showers of Blessings Church.

Author Contact – PhyllisNThomas@gmail.com

www.ingramcontent.com/pod-product-compliance
Lightning Source LLC
Chambersburg PA
CBHW062030040426
42447CB00010B/2216